Offered Up to Be Set Apart

Offered Up to Be Set Apart

When Love Choose You Victory is Assured

By: D. Jones

XULON PRESS

Xulon Press
2301 Lucien Way #415
Maitland, FL 32751
407.339.4217
www.xulonpress.com

© 2020 by D. Jones

All rights reserved solely by the author. The author guarantees all contents are original and do not infringe upon the legal rights of any other person or work. No part of this book may be reproduced in any form without the permission of the author. The views expressed in this book are not necessarily those of the publisher.

Unless otherwise indicated, Scripture quotations taken from the Holy Bible, New International Version (NIV). Copyright © 1973, 1978, 1984, 2011 by Biblica, Inc.™. Used by permission. All rights reserved.

Printed in the United States of America.

ISBN-13: 978-1-6312-9211-8

❀❀❀❀❀❀❀❀❀❀❀

I dedicate this book to *You. T*he modern Job of this decade. The person who has felt like life has been a series of misfortunate, heartache, and pain and has left you asking the question "Why me?" I pray this book will answer your "why?," provide healing, propel you into your purpose, and that you will draw closer to God, the Father, through our Lord and Savior Jesus Christ. Life is serious at times, and hope can seem faint. I pray that you will read my testimony and regain your hope in Christ and walk in obedient faith.

I also dedicate this book to my family—my mother; aunts; uncles; cousins; the entire Jones family, who always supported me, accepted me, and encouraged me to do whatever God placed in my heart.

Finally, I dedicate this book to my children, Tee, Monte, Christopher (Deuce, in heaven), and Zee. My grandchildren, Ziya (Cupcake) and Trevoy (Sweet Daddy). I love y'all to the very depths of my being and thank you for being great kids. Your destiny is so great, just remain in Christ because your steps are ordered.

CONTENTS

Introduction ix

Chapter 1: So Many Plans 1

Chapter 2: What I Feared The Most 13

Chapter 3: Dark and Hard Places........................... 19

Chapter 4: The Offer.. 33

Chapter 5: Burying Dead Things 41

Chapter 6: Set Apart.. 49

Chapter 7: Victory is Assured -We Win 55

Journal Your Process 65

Acknowledgements 69

Reference 71

Introduction

I would first like to state that my experience and expertise come from Hard-knocks University. This university has offered degrees to most of us. This book is not to substitute any books you may be reading about self-help. This book was inspired by the Holy Spirit within me to tell the testimonies of my life, in hopes that it will deliver, inspire, and propel you into the promises of God. The contents of this book were hard to relive and discuss, but I know it is much needed in the world we live in. Even as I finish writing this book, I have not yet stopped experiencing life and being taught by its lessons. I have not arrived at knowing all or most of anything. However, I'm in pursuit of what God has for me.

I'm praying that as you turn the pages, each word will seep into your heart, renew your mind, and bless your soul. Take a deep breath and prepare yourself, as I take you through the events that have change and are currently changing my life, in hopes that you will see that if I was offered up for something greater, so were you, and God's promises cannot be voided.

Chapter 1: So Many Plans

Jeremiah 29:11 KJV
For I know the thoughts that I think toward you, saith the Lord, thoughts of peace, and not of evil, to give you an expected end.

Jeremiah 29:10-11 The Message (MSG)
This is God's Word on the subject: "As soon as Babylon's seventy years are up and not a day before, I'll show up and take care of you as I promised and bring you back home. I know what I'm doing. I have it all planned out—plans to take care of you, not abandon you, plans to give you the future you hope for."

As a child, I dreamed of becoming a doctor. To be specific, I wanted to become an obstetrician-gynecologist. The plan was to graduate from high school, attend Texas Christian University, then attend University of Texas Southwestern Medical School. After graduating from medical school, I would start my private practice that would specialize in teenage pregnancy with combination of mentoring young teens. After I was successful in business, I would marry and have a total of five kids, buy acres of land, and build a dream home with lots of animals. I bet you are now wondering which part of these plans really happen. Well, not all of them happen. Could they have happened? Yes. Instead, I choose a path that was contrary to my dreams. When we are inexperienced and young, we don't fully understand how small decisions lead to huge shifts in our lives and consequences. But, we must ask, are they really consequences, or were they part of God's plan? Did God know that I would choose wrong? Did I surprise God?

Not Even I Was Exempt

The tragedies begin as soon as I entered the world.

I wss born to a teenager mother in her last year of high school, as soon as I came out the birth canal, my mom and I stop breathing. The nurses and doctors worked frantically to revive us. My mom began to bleed profusely, and to stop the blood, she had to receive a full hysterectomy which caused her to be barren the remainder of her life. We both survived. Only time would tell how many near-death experiences and the fight for life I would endure.

Around the age of four, we lived in an area we called Rolling Hills. When it would storm or rain hard, the power in the area would be affected by blackouts. One stormy evening, the lights went out. To entertain ourselves, my cousin and I decided to play our cat and mouse game with the illumination of only candles burning throughout our house. I had long, thick curly hair, and it just so happens my mom had recently washed it, so it was like a curly afro all over my head. He was pretending that he was the cat and began to chase me.

During this fun game, I ran too close to one of the candles and *poof!* That's right. My hair caught on fire. Well, in a panic, my mom poured a bucket of water on me. If the fire didn't try to kill me, the bucket of water almost did. We all were hysterical. The fire consumed almost 60 percent of my hair and burned the majority of one my ears. I guess taking your kid to the hospital was not the norm back then, only home remedies. My great grandmother lived with us and had so many plants.

One of them, luckily was an aloe vera plant. Needless to say, the properties of the aloe vera plant healed me and grew my hair back. I'm by no means endorsing aloe vera as a primary treatment for burns, but only telling you what happen in my life. My mom would wash my hair and scalp with it every day. The home remedy worked so well, the burned side of my hair grew past the unaffected part. I played the burn victim well; I wouldn't walk, and if I did, I would walk with my head tilted to one side as though my neck was injured. I was something else. Now, all these incidents happened before I turned seven years of age, and I'm only highlighting just a few of them.

Our family suffered a great loss on November 27, 1987, when my grandfather passed away. It took a toll on each one of us differently. I had never met a man that was so generous, patient, loving, kind, and who so loved the Lord. He was our father mixed with being a grandfather. My cousin and I were the only two grandchildren at the time. He raised us as his very own. He taught us everything from taking care of animals and counting money, to building a treehouse. I would watch him pray for the family, and he would place his hand on my back at times when he prayed in front of me. Every Sunday, Tuesday, Wednesday, and Saturday, we were at church for some type of service. We were raised to put God first, but at the time, we didn't know why we were made to go to church. We just knew we never had a choice in the matter.

My grandfather was family-oriented and believed that family should stick together no matter what. God had blessed him with a gift of singing. I would hear him singing each Sunday mornings as he got ready for church. He was absolutely wonderful. Our family lost the glue that held everything together when he died. But God was so merciful, and He continued to allow us to grow as a family. My grandmother became the matriarch of the family, and she did her best to keep our holiday traditions going. However, she had her own struggles, with her mom, my great-grandmother, who living with us throughout her marriage and with picking up the pieces of her duties. She was left the figure out life on her own after her husband, and then her mother, passed away.

My grandmother was very spoiled and used to getting her way. I can't remember anyone ever telling her no. She always expected everyone to listen to her and do as she said, regardless of our thoughts and feelings towards it.

By the age of nine, my mom moved to the west side of the city due to work. My grandmother was very attached to me, and she bullied my mom into allowing me to live with her and my great-grandmother. My great-grandmother wasn't very nice, but I suspected that was because she was sick and tired of being sick. However, during her harsh discussions, she would make me get a Bible and read passages and remember the books of the Bible. I would have to recite the books of the Bible between commercials while she sat in her bed, watching wrestling.

My grandmother was a very strong-willed woman, and she ruled our entire family after my grandfather passed away. She was loving towards me, but she had anger with others. My great-grandmother became ill and passed, so my grandmother moved a family friend in to live with us. Every evening they would go to the bingo hall to play bingo until late at night while I was left at home. He was a nice friend to my grandmother, until one day he decided he didn't want to go to bingo, and she went by herself. This was the day the innocence of my childhood was ruined. He started molesting me until I was eventually raped by someone else. I could have told someone, but during that time, I was left alone to handle myself, and I felt so disguised, ruined, and embarrassed even at ten or eleven years of age. What my grandmother feared would happen if I stayed at home alone while my mother worked happened by her bringing darkness into her own home. Even then, I knew I couldn't tell her what she feared had come upon her. I knew telling her and my mom would crushed them; their protection was more important than what I had endured.

By the time I was thirteen years of age, I hadn't been raised by anyone specifically. I just grew to model what I saw. My mom was a church worshipper, respectful, kind, timid, and passive in her ways and giving. My oldest aunt, the oldest of my mom's siblings, was the respectful mother-figure to all in the family. She was genuine, full of wisdom, hard-working, well-traveled, and carried herself with dignity. Next was my youngest aunt; she was aggressive, opinionated, boisterous, good with money, and trendy. All the women were good housekeepers, even my grandmothers. I just picked and chose what I wanted to model from each one of them. The only father figures I had at the time was my uncles who both were workaholics, and they treated me as their daughters the best way they could.

All the adults, however, were caught up in their lives and immediate responsibilities, so during my early adolescent, I often felt I wasn't anyone's first priority. I was literally doing whatever I wanted. I was driving a Jeep tracker to middle school, and when I moved around for a few years, I didn't have a curfew when I wasn't with my immediate family. I moved in with my cousin, whose mom was never at home due to her being a nurse.

By the summer of 1994, I was fifteen years old and hanging out with cousins and friends, cutting up drugs, making drugs, and hanging with gangs and we went where ever we wanted to go. I was driving drugs to Houston. I was dating a guy, but he was much older than I and was doing the same thing I was doing, just on a larger level. I didn't have to worry about the sexual contact all the time, because our focus was making money. However, when I was fifteen years of age, I met the father of my oldest kids. He was older also, nice, but very controlling which led to very abusive behavior. I saw signs from the very first time we met. But since I didn't have my own personal relationship with my father, I mistook his controlling ways for love. I felt, at the time, he must really love me to control my whereabouts and what I wear.

By the age of sixteen, I had my first child. She is my first real love. She was so sweet, and she provided a love that I had never experienced before: unconditional love. She just loves her mama despite my faults, and I just knew I had to do better by her and myself. That's when I decided I couldn't do the illegal things I had been involved in such as street hustling. I got a job at a call center and worked part-time at a hotel answering phones. I went to night school to get my high school diploma and then got another weekend job. By the time I was seventeen years old, I had my own apartment and my own car. I worked very hard to keep and maintain it to make sure I didn't get any government assistance. I didn't want to be another young female in the system, making other taxpayers pay for my poor decision making. I wanted to give my child the best opportunity and show her that with hard work and God, you can obtain anything. But in working hard and raising her, I entered adult life very early and neglected myself and that made me vulnerable in seeking love.

I had two kids by the abusive ex, my only complete break away came by the death of my best friend, who was murdered by her ex-boyfriend. She was one of the closest people I had to a sister. I spent the majority of my summers with her and her family in the country when I was younger. Back then, they were one of the first black families in this small country town, so we experienced life lessons. The death of my friend/sister shifted my way of thinking. I knew my situation could end the same if I didn't disconnect from my current boyfriend. Death of loved ones was very familiar to me at this point in life. And although my plans of marrying my abusive ex were thrown, I created a new set of plans. Now, my new plans were to get a home, a good job, and be able to take care of my kids on a higher level of living. My oldest kids' father did not share in a lot of the financial responsibility, nor did he spend time with my kids. I often wonder what thoughts he carried in his mind about his decisions. I realized early on that his decision were based not only in his personal choice, but in a generational curse as well. His father was never in his life. His mother also grew up as a single mother raising three children. Sometimes, our decisions are not necessary our decisions, sometimes choices are based on limited thinking and cultural concepts that leave consequences in the background of our decisions. My thoughts towards him are humbling and merciful. I prayed for him while raising my kids that he would make the right decisions, and I would tell my kids to love him regardless because the way he perceives life may be different from our thinking and to allow God to work out his heart and judge him accordingly.

The father of my first two children and I had been separated for 6 months when my mother introduced me to this guy. She didn't know much about him, but he was respectful towards her. He is the father of my second son (my third kid). He didn't have a two-parent family as well, and his grandmother raised him with the best knowledge she had. He was a decent guy, but he had a street mentality, which I was drawn too. That happens when what hasn't died within you drives you to find what is compatible in another person. I too had known the streets. He only knew how to live by street rules, or as we say in my culture the hood. I had grown out of the lifestyle, but I wasn't judgmental about others who were still in it. Our relationship came to an end abruptly, after my encounter with God.

My oldest cousin invited me to church with him a couple of blocks from my aunt's home. This small white wood frame church sat in between residential areas. I didn't expect this moment to be the turning point of all of my meaningless plans. The pastor was a young guy who had just begun ministry, and he began to preach about the righteousness of God and how God can change everything in your life around. I grew up in church and knew who God was but didn't quite have a relationship with God. I would only talk to Him or pray when I was begging for Him to get me out of trouble, asking Him to bless me, or asking Him to protect me. My relationship with God was one-sided. I'm ashamed to say, He was my side-dude. Everyone else was the main person. I spent just enough time with Him to keep Him relevant in my life.

However, on this particular day, the preacher said something that would awaken a spirit that had been lying dormant in me. I remember crying out to God to deliver me from whatever was hindering me. Immediately, I felt a twinkling in my heart and lightness come over me; a feeling of joy and hope overwhelmed me, as though God had a plan for this very moment and it finally came to pass. I was living with my son's father, and I knew at that moment everything had to come to an end because it made be vulnerable to sin, such as lust for sex. I started seeing my life and my children life totally different. I finally understood my life so far had been below the standards God had set for my life. I remember telling my son's father to leave one day because God couldn't do what He needed to do in my life fully if he remained there with me without changing his ways and being married. He left and I felt the fullness of God come in. I didn't have much money, but I had a lot of God. I had peace. The best feeling in the world is to be full of Him because nothing can take Him away from us (neither death or life). Now getting the courage to tell my son's father to leave was a hard task and very uncomfortable. He was bringing money into our home, and he was a good guy making bad decisions. I wanted to know how it felt to put God first before others. This was not my plan, but only what had been written before the time. But, when I thought everything was moving smoothly, something huge would come to throw me for a loop.

A Horrible Car Accident

It was a Tuesday evening, and I was coming home from work, heading to apply for a second part-time job. I was driving down a four-lane street in a busy area; it was during rush hour traffic when everyone was trying to get home from work. Well, as I was driving, I could see a man from a distance standing on the yellow line that divides the incoming and outcoming lances. My first thought was, *Please don't let this man try to cross lanes, and please don't let him get hit.* But before I could send up a prayer or process that last thought, he decided to cross the busy intersection. A truck traveling northbound hit the man and tossed him more than twenty-five feet in the air towards my car, as I was traveling southbound. All I could see was this human being in the air, coming directing towards me. He hit my windshield and bounced off my car. I could hear his body hit the pavement, and I felt my car run over his body. In a panic, I quickly pulled over, jumped out the car ,and ran into the middle of the street where his body was lifeless and shaking. The police officers who had been parked at a restaurant nearby saw the entire incident, so they ran into the middle of the street to grab me because cars were slamming on their brakes to avoid hitting all of us in the middle of the street. The only thing I could see was this older man's body with wound to his head open and blood everywhere; brain fragments and tissue was spattered. I was so hysterical when the ambulance came, they took me to the hospital for elevated blood pressure. I couldn't stop screaming and wailing. It was so terrifying.

The nice police officers took my car after the investigation was completed and detailed it. They drove my car to my home. I was so frightened, I didn't want to drive for a while. I began to have serious nightmares of bodies coming through my house windows, and I would see headless men walking around my house. It was so bad, my uncle (who was a pastor) would come and stay with me so that I could have some peace. I would call him often hysterical because I didn't know how to get past what I saw. My uncle would come and pray for me and over my house. At the time, I thought that was one of the most horrible tragedies to happened to me. I had experienced death, rape, molestation, and other car incidents, but nothing of this magnitude.

Things got better over time, and I ended up marrying my friend from work. I became pregnant with my second daughter. Now, I have a total of four kids. It all happened so quickly. This may sound great for a husband-seeker, but it is not good for a Christ-seeker. It was still not in God's plan; it was my plan, by the direction of a family member who influenced me to get married because I was pregnant and already had kids. I was listening to what made sense from myself and others, but not listening to God. I believed Jesus Christ is the son of God, but I hadn't allowed Him to be Lord over my life. I was still trying to control everything. I didn't fully understand Psalm 23:1, "The Lord is my shepherd." When Jesus is Lord over our lives, He gives us orders, and we should follow without doubting, just fully trusting him. Many Christians like myself think that when they became born again, their decisions or plans would automatically be blessed by God, even if they never consult Him first. He is the Leader in the game called Simon Says. When we don't follow Him, we make decisions that give consequences that could have been avoided. Here is another piece of my life story to show how doing things my way didn't make the cut.

My Marriage My Way

My husband at the time was a great, but he had his own baggage dealing with his family. He was a wonderful friend, but being good friends don't always make for great marriages. People come into your life for seasons and reasons, and the reasons can be tainted if we are not following God's plan. My reason for marrying him was tainted, as was his reason for marrying me. I wanted a husband because the older people told me I needed one to help raise my kids, I enjoyed calling someone my husband, and I liked the title of being a wife and the duties of a wife. I didn't know the foundation of marriage like the love of a wife towards her husband. I wasn't ready for marriage because I didn't even know myself and what type of man I needed. I didn't know the order is for a husband to seek out a wife with God's purpose in mind. He felt the same way, but, at the time, marriage sounded like a good idea. It wasn't a good idea for us, though. We learned the hard way. We both had great jobs and made good money, but we created many bills.

God did get glory from our marriage because He blessed us with a daughter. We didn't bare any good fruit but her. A good way to know if you are sowing into good ground is by the fruit it bears. Our marriage was barren. We both loved God, but our union was not of God. We experience several family issues that caused a rift in our immediate family and resulted in our marriage being strained. Even with this, I didn't know what would follow. I just knew what I had planned so far was a lot to bear with only a little progress in my eyes. We did experience good times with our kid and cousins we help raised, but that was all of it.

Never in a million years did I know what God had in store for me in years to come. Sometimes, I wonder if I would have wanted God to tell me His plans for my life, so I would have been better prepared. Then I realized, maybe God didn't want to hear me kicking and screaming for years to come. At that point in my life, I just knew God had me on His mind and that was good enough for me. But absolutely nothing could have prepared me for what was coming next.

Chapter 2: What I Feared The Most

Job 3:25-26 King James Version (KJV) For the thing which I greatly feared is come upon me, and that which I was afraid of is come unto me. I was not in safety, neither had I rest, neither was I quiet; yet trouble came.

Job 3:25-26 The Message (MSG) Instead of bread I get groans for my supper, then leave the table and vomit my anguish. The worst of my fears has come true, what I've dreaded most has happened. My repose is shattered, my peace destroyed. No rest for me, ever—death has invaded life.

February 14, 2005, Valentine's Day. A day of love and admiration, and the gathering of love amongst most people. However, this day started out for me as being a day of hell, horror, and death. A day of destruction. This is what I assumed at first, but what led to this day?

February 13, 2005. When my youngest son returned home from his father's for the weekend, it was a day like every other day. When he walked through the door, he was full of stories of how he celebrated the weekend of his father. He followed me to my bedroom, as I was reorganizing my closet. He continue to tell me about everything a four-year-old's mind had on it. He went from one subject to the next as I listened, questioned, and answered a series of questions. By the time he had reached his hundredth question, he became very quiet after I answered his. I turned to see what he was doing, and he had talked himself into a nap on my floor with his Incredible Hulk shirt and sweatpants on. So, I just covered him up with a blanket and continued to let him rest. I thought to myself, *He must have had a long weekend,* because it was early in the afternoon, and he was completely in a deep sleep, snoring and slobbering at the mouth. I finished organizing my closet, and then I woke him up so he could get ready for school the next day along with his sibling.

Every Sunday, there was a schedule that started around 8 a.m. It was schedule that we had followed for years. We would get up and eat breakfast, go to church, eat dinner after church, take a small nap, prepare clothes for the week for school and work, the baths and bedtime by 8:00-8:30 p.m. for the kids. Everything was on schedule so far, until my oldest daughter told me at the last minute she had to do a project for school. This caused an issue with the usual rotation of bath time. Normally , my oldest daughter would bathe first, then my two sons, then I would bathe my baby girl. The boys always took a bath together: they were only one year apart and they enjoyed playing with toys in the bathtub.

I went into their room and told them, how the bath rotation would go this day. I said, "Well, kids, change of plans. Boys, y'all go first to bathe, then your sister will take a bath last so she can finish her school project." I ran the bath water to start their bath. But youngest son, Deuce, made an announcement: he didn't want to bathe with my other son because he said he would urinate in the water. So, he refused to take another bath with his brother. I agreed. I said, "Well, you get in first, and then he will get in." As he got into the water, he began to tell me how excited about Valentine's Day the next day. He was so excited that he wanted me to let him taste test the cupcakes I had purchased for his class at breakfast the next day. I said, "Deuce, that wouldn't be a good idea for me to give you a cupcake at breakfast. That would upset your stomach along with your teacher due to the sugar rush." Deuce replied, "Mama, she don't care." I told him that, yes, his teacher would mind, since he had rarely received a good green happy face since attending school. I was afraid what color face he would receive with sugar being the driving force. We talked briefly, then he paused as he saw me exiting the bathroom, and he said, "Mama, I love you." I told him I loved him too.

I called out for my daughter to meet me in my room so we could start her project. As we entered by room, my husband at the time was entering our master bathroom to take a shower. My daughter and I sat on the bed and started her project, maybe a few minutes later, he called out from the bathroom that someone was running water somewhere in the house, because his shower water had turned cold. I told my daughter to run the bathroom where my son was at and tell him to get out of the tub. When she returned, she said he had turned the water on because his water had cooled and he wanted it hot, but he was getting out now. So I continued helping her with her project for a few more minutes before I sent her on her way to her room and to take her bath.

The next few minutes changed my entire life, as my daughter ran back into my room, screaming, saying something about Deuce. The only thing I could do was respond to her screaming and run to the front of the house. When I got to the hallway, I saw my lifeless baby boy laying their naked. What do you do when you see your future laying down dying? I immediately started CPR, and my husband called 911. All I could hear a few moments were screams from my other children, but my mind isolated the noises, and I only could focus on feeling the breath of life coming out of my son's body every time I tried to breathe life into him. His eyes were set glazed at someone that I couldn't see, but I could feel. As I cried out to God, to please let him stay and to take me, I could feel that my requests were not being granted.

The emergency responders rushed in and took Deuce's body and started conducting their CPR. I got in the Medic with him. They worked diligently all the way to the hospital, and when we finally arrived— after a drive that seem like it took four days—we entered the hospital doors, and they took him into a different room that I couldn't enter. Then, I heard a loud voice say, "Oh my God! The tube was placed down the wrong pipe in his throat," and then the doors were closed in front of me. They took me into this room, where my other kids' father and his mother were waiting.

After a while, a detective walked in and started asking me questions about what happened, and she advised that she had already been at our home and talked to my others kids. She told me freak accidents happen, and he was old enough to bathe by himself but he had added more water to the tub and his siblings had told her what happen in terms of where everyone was at. I was so hysterical; I couldn't stop screaming and crying as I sat myself on the floor of this room. The detective woman got on the floor with me and just hugged me for a duration that seem for hours as she wept. The doctors finally came and got me from the room and told me they had taken Deuce to ICU, and they were running test to determine how much damage had been done.

At this time, the word had spread of what happened, so the hospital was full of people from family to friends to coworkers to spectators. As I walked into his room, I saw my baby's body hooked up to these machines with a diaper on as though he was in a deep sleep. Every few hours, doctor after doctor would come in telling us what they were doing to him and which tests were coming back. Each test that came back was not in our favor. I finally told the doctors to keep running the tests for any chance of hope. I walked into the waiting room where I saw so many people, but I was looking amongst the people for strength.

I found my uncle who was a pastor sitting in the back of the room, I went and sat directly by him. He began to tell me not to worry, everything would be ok, and Deuce would live. But in my spirit, I knew it was not so. I told my uncle, "He is gone."

He replied "Don't say that. He will live."

I said, as broken as I have been ever in my life, "He left when he was on the floor of the house."

Deuce's father arrived from out of town, and the doctors told us we had to make a decision of whether to take him off life support. His father and I walked outside the hospital and discussed it, but the decision was mine alone since I had primary custody.

At 2:30 p.m. on February 14, 2005, my baby boy Christopher, at the age of four years old and one month from turning five years old, was pronounced dead. When the life support machine was removed, I completely felt as though someone had unplugged the cord on my mind, heart, and existence. All the prayers I prayed since I was a child, since my kids were born, and during the duration of their life seem to have been pointless. All the Bible reading, seeking God, loving God, trying to live by God's standards, getting baptized, treating others right, and paying tithes and offering seemed so worthless. The anger increased when I realized a little boy the same age in the next room had lived, after he had swallowed grams of crack cocaine while his parents sold drugs in the next room.

I began to ask God in confusion, "How can this be? I loved my kids, cared for them with all my being. I had sacrificed, worked two and three jobs, taught them about You, told them to trust You, and You left us. You abandon us; now the enemy has consumed us." I told God, "I did everything I knew that was required of me. Yes, I made mistakes, but I repented, and You gave me another chance." Now, this happened. I felt like Jesus did on the cross. I could connect on a lower scale how Jesus felt on the cross, when He cried out, "Father, Father, why how thou forsaken me?" (Matt 27:46) Jesus must have felt God had turned away from Him. I felt the same way. I understood I had not been perfect all my life and that I was a sinner, but at that moment of my life, I was saved by the death, burial, and resurrection of Christ. I knew my past mistakes were covered under the blood, and now this. What do you do when you feel like what you have been serving has failed you? What I had feared the most since I was sixteen and having my first baby, I had come upon. This was my greatest fear.

Chapter 3: Dark and Hard Places

John 1:5
The light shines in the darkness, and the darkness can never extinguish it.

Voice in Pain

I entered the waiting room that was jammed packed with family, friends, co-workers, onlookers, and haters. As I stood in the middle of the waiting room, I announced my son had passed away. I remember hearing screams, loud outbursts, and people dropping to the floor due to grief. I almost fainted after I announced it, so I had to take a seat. I then got up from my seat and walked down to the chapel of the hospital. When I arrived at the door of the chapel, I felt like I was finding refuge from the pain of the worst news I had ever received. I entered the chapel, and no one was in there, just empty seats and an empty altar. I went to the front were I could imagine the altar of God would be in heaven, and I just fell on the floor right there as my voice exclaimed with screams that came from the bottom of my soul. The screams that projected out of my mouth were a sound I couldn't even imagine my body could produce. I screamed and cried asking God, "Why me? Why my son?" The Holy Spirit, in His soft voice, told me to remember His servant Job. I said, "Lord, I need to know why, right now." The Holy Spirit just came, telling me to remember Job.

I laid there, because that was the only place I knew to go. I knew in my heart. I had to go back to God, with myself being open to Him. I was furious, hurt, in so much pain, disappointed, and wanted answers. At the altar, I wept uncontrollably, pleaded for a Lazarus miracle, and asked for understanding repeatedly. Every part of my being was crying out to God. My flesh felt faint, trembling, and my soul was saddened beyond belief, my spirit felt as though it was being torn apart. I'm not sure if you have been in this place in your life. A place of complete darkness. There was no silver lining, no cup half-full, none of the nonsense my intellect could conjure up. A place where direction can't be found. This place of darkness is so intense, you have to just sit still and release control in the place you're in. A place where no visitors come nor are visitors welcomed . This place is totally dark, where dead things live and where life doesn't exist.

Suddenly, a quiet voice of peace and comfort was heard in the place of darkness I sat in. I could feel a hand on my shoulder; I could feel someone with me that knew the pain I was experiencing. This presence that showed up suddenly and knew me. I could feel we had so much in common. I could feel that this being had been through this before. In my pain, the voice said, "I am here. " I am the one from the beginning. I am the one that would be here to the very end." My spirit in Him connected like no other time in my life. The Spirit of God began to remind me saying, "I remember giving up my son for you; it hurt me, but I knew you would have to come through this."

We began to communicate, and my soul cried out, "I cannot take this pain."

The voice in my Spirit then said, "You don't have to be alone, just rest in Me."

I asked, "God, what did I do wrong?"

The Spirit of God would say, "I have ordered your steps, you shall live and not die."

Everything my soul cried out, but the Spirit of God would remind me of His Word until He said again, "Remember my servant Job." I didn't know what remember Job meant, but it stuck with me, and peace began to rise up in me, pressing through my flesh of hurt. I was able to at least stand up again on feet that I was unsure of.

When Hearts Are Harden

When I returned to the visiting area, CPS and a police detective were there. The detective concluded that the incident was an accident with no neglect found. But because I was so hysterical at the hospital, they felt I would commit suicide over my son's death, so they told my family to take care of my other kids while I processed my son dying. The detective feared that I would commit suicide and my kids would find me. My kids went to stay with my parents, and my stepsister helped with my infant daughter. My husband and I went to stay with my aunt and uncle because I refused to go back to my house where my son's accident happen. The detective came over to the house where I was staying and told me she was prayed for me.

I didn't know that even though the police and CPS had closed their case immediately, an interrogation amongst friends and families would begin. People at work were holding court trials about me, and I wasn't there to defend myself. Several family members started questioning me about what happened on different days as though I was lying. They were questioning my kids as if they were the police. People were calling the detective on the case, demanding that the case be reopened, saying that I didn't hurt my son, but maybe my other children did because he was light-skinned with blue eyes and they were jealous. My other kids were eight, five, and one at the time. I couldn't mourn my son because I had to protect my other kids from the vicious attacks of adults. The hurt from my son passing increased. When I thought family and friends would support me, some weren't available. I looked around and saw only a few that I could connect with and on God to comfort and help me.

Offered Up to Be Set Apart

The planning of the funeral was extremely hard. Luckily, my aunt was a manager of the funeral home, and she managed the funeral entirely. My first viewing of my son was like seeing a piece of myself in the casket. All I could see was one of the most beautiful gifts God had blessed me with; he had been so full of life, and now I was burying my purest love I had ever experienced to never regain it again in this life. It took my breath away. As I looked at him, I was telling God in my heart, *Father, I will take his place.* I saw his lifeless body lying in a casket, and I would see it no more. He was perfectly imperfect. He was my baby. Born to me, for me. After leaving the funeral home after the first viewing, I didn't feel like a mother any longer.

At the funeral, I felt sick, and I felt like I was having an out-of-body experience. It was as though I was in a bad nightmare that never would end. I had saw him, in the casket, days before; I had seen his lifeless body dressed in his normal clothing, a basketball jersey, baseball cap, and denim jeans his father had bought him. But to see the casket again, unopened, just did something to me. I felt weak, like a failure, and completely empty. As all the thoughts were going through my mind, I couldn't hear what was being said after the prayer. I was so numb that I felt as though I was a walking zombie.

It wasn't until I heard a woman's voice on the microphone that I could focus. It sounded so clear and concise as it told a story about David and Bathsheba. The voice emphasized how God had taken their child because of the sin of the parents. I sunk into total humiliation. I just put my head down in shame and cried uncontrollably from the inside out because now, at my son's funeral, I was being told that God took my son because of my sin. Tension rose, and most of my family got up and left the church pews to prevent from exploding. My uncle was the officiant pastor, and he took over and told me from the pulpit to hold my head up high because God doesn't make any mistakes. But at the time, it was so unbearable, I wanted to crawl into the casket with my son. It was too much to bear for one person. After all, this was my greatest fear. What I had feared the most was now my reality.

Experiencing what I feared the most didn't keep tragedies from continuing to happen. I thought feeling abandoned, being raped and molested, losing my best friend, a deadly car accident, and now losing my son was enough for a twenty-five year old woman. Life didn't stop though, and people didn't stop. It was the one thing that had wounded my soul the deepest. It was the pinnacle point of things that would happen in my life. So, you are reading this and probably thinking, *Oh my God, what else could happen to one person?* A lot! I was just giving you the introduction of my life. I'm just setting the stage for you to get a complete understanding, so it can minister to your life by my testimonies. You are not alone in devastation, despair, pain, and brokenness.

The dark place was a very hard place. After I buried my son, I received a six-page letter in the mail from a relative through marriage, explaining how she had been praying that I would die and the rest of my kids also. She explained in the letter that she had been begging God to take my life. Several things similar to this happened, but after this, I couldn't take any more, and my husband at the time had an obligation to take care of his grandmother. So these circumstances, along with other things, led up to us getting a divorce. We remained friends and co-parents afterwards.

I didn't realize that I was still a shell of a person. I was in a deep state of denial. I kept myself busy with work, my kids, everything I could think of to keep my mind off of the pain that was growing daily. Then, one day, I met a guy, and we became friends even though we were different. I needed someone to save since I didn't feel like I had saved my son. He didn't have a great job, but he had a heart for God, so I prayed. God showed me signs and, through prayer, told me not to marry him because his agenda would only benefit him. I didn't listen. Out of my brokenness, I wanted to save someone. I married him. I discovered after we were married that he was bipolar which led to him not keeping jobs. So, I carried the weight of our life by myself the majority of the time. Not only was I trying to save him, I was trying to prove to myself that I could be great at something, since I failed as a mother. So, I paid every bill, paid off his past bills, and helped him get his commercial driver's license (CDL) to do better for himself.

Then, in 2010, after my step-father passed away, my body finally responded to my internal pain. My body broke itself to cause me to rest. I had a stroke at the age of thirty years old. I had just answered the call to minister to God's people, and now I would be in the hospital suffering from a stroke. It happened while I was I driving home from work, and I was talking to my uncle on my cell phone. All of a sudden, my left side went completely out; there was no movement, and I couldn't think of how to say I needed help. My uncle was asking me questions, but I was mumbling because I couldn't speak. He told me to try to calm down and pull over. I immediately stopped my car and called 911. When I got to the hospital, after many tests, they determined I had a stroke, and I needed to stay. My family was in disbelief and very sensitive because we had just buried a family member. I was afraid. I couldn't talk properly, and I couldn't walk using my left side or use my left arm properly. My body had finally taken a vacation and never asked me.

When I finally got home from the hospital, my husband shut down on me totally. I asked him why he was so distant and was barely helping me. He told me, "God should have killed you, because I never signed up to be with someone that would get sick." I just couldn't believe it. He had a hard time keeping a job, so to offset his lack, I would work two or three jobs to fill in the gaps while never complaining. Once I was healed, I started back ministering, and he would get upset because he felt as though I got a better response from ministering than he did. I forgot to tell you, he was a minister also.

The truth is, *I never* wanted to be up in front of anyone. I just wanted to pray from the pews. My desire was never to speak to a crowd of people, I just wanted to see people healed and set free by God's Word. I didn't need nor want the attention, but I knew I had to say what was on my heart from God to say. I would be crying to keep from going up there because I didn't want to disappoint God. My husband saw how I struggled with stage fright as well, but it didn't matter. The jealous grew stronger. I keep praying it would get better, but I was reminded in how I said, "no," to God from the beginning to teaching and ministering to his people. He would withhold affection towards me as punishment if he was upset for any reason. I constantly felt rejected, and I would constantly ask if I did anything wrong. I know he didn't look at himself in a healthy way, so I was his emotional punching bag.

However, once he landed a great job after getting his CDL, I thought everything would change due to him making more money and this would help his insecurities. But, before he could even receive his first paycheck, he came home and told me that he doesn't need a woman to help him now, and instantly, something broke in my spirit. I was crushed. I began to explain how I had worked part-time to pay thousands of dollars' worth of traffic tickets, made his child support payments, and would still manage the duties as a wife, and my reward was that he was never interested in being a team with me. What God had revealed from the beginning was the truth. I remember God would tell me through the marriage that my husband didn't value me.

So, one day I had a vision. I was driving on my way to work and in the middle of the freeway was a large, wrapped gift. Everyone was driving around it, trying not to hit it. But this one car passed by me with my husband driving, and he ran right into the corner of the gift intentionally. But then, this guy jumped out a car and ran in the middle of the freeway and picked it up. So, I came home and told my husband about the vision I had. He responded and said, "Oh, you think you are a gift to me? Yeah right." I didn't respond because, in that moment, the Holy Spirit revealed that my husband would leave. Now, I didn't know how or when. I just knew he was leaving.

Then one day, my husband had a bad day at work, so I came home to him sitting on the side of the bed eating dinner. When I walked in, I saw a folded army-style knife lying on the dresser, but I didn't pay it much attention. As I sat on the bed, he began to text me. I responded by asking him why he was texting me when I was in the room with him. He stated that was the only time he could talk to me by text, which was weird because I called him on every break and lunch at work. So, I responded, "Whatever," because I could sense argument coming. Then, the next thing I knew, he was over me, waving a knife in the air, trying to stab me, but he accidentally stabbed himself.

After this incident, he moved all his things that very same day and never returned. He later told me that God had warn him, that if he didn't treat me right, He would remove him, and he didn't listen. I never told him to leave or said a word during this incident. He just left on his own. I forgave him, and we filed for a divorce and decided to be friends. God knew this wasn't the marriage for me. I know that marriage is of God and is honorable. I realize sometimes we enter covenants with people without consulting God at all, or we consult Him and still want to do it our way despite what He says.

Afterwards, I dated a guy; he was nice and someone I was familiar with from middle school, but we were on different paths in life. We decided to be friends. However, during this time, I realized I wasn't ok. I wasn't healed. I was a very broken person. I had never been to the cemetery for my son. I had started having very bad migraines and seizures after my stroke, and they had increased during this time of my life. The doctor had told me on October 22, 2017, that he was going to suspend my license because I had several episodes of driving and not knowing where I was or episodes of being somewhere and not knowing how to get back to my car due to the seizures. This was devastating news. I had been through so much, and all I had left was working and running my remodeling business. I felt like I wouldn't benefit the world if I couldn't produce. I could feel everything from the past thirty-eight years piling on me, and I was sinking into a dark place that I didn't think even God could see me in. So, I decided on October 26, 2017 to go to the cemetery, and that's when it happened. Reality told me I'm not superwoman, I failed as a mother, and I can't do this life.

Chapter 3: Dark And Hard Places

The Suicide

I titled this chapter "Dark and Hard Places" because, throughout my life, I have landed in a hard place called rock bottom. This place I was currently in was no different in terms of trials, but it was different in terms of essence. I had gone through thirty-seven years, almost two months shy of turning thirty-eight, of ups and downs. Trial after trial. We can call trials attacks on one's life. I have given a lot over the years, emotionally, financially, and physically. I had completely drained myself out, even when God had given me so many ways for restorations. I had to sacrifice for people who I truly loved and loved me back, and I also did it for some who didn't love me back.

But everything came to an end October 26, 2017. All week, I had been having partial seizures which caused me to be very tired and my vision to be different. I had had a seizure every day that week and was having problems sleeping. But, I was still pushing myself to maintain my household and business and to help others with anything they needed. I felt like my body was going to pass out at any moment. I don't know if my body was so tired that it started prompting these dreams of me having a stroke repeatedly. That morning felt different for me. I wasn't in a good space. I can't describe it. It was very dark and lonely. Mentally, I had just even up. So, I was at work talking to my friend about issues and business, and I just checked out mentally.

I got up from the table and went to my car. I drove the park and just decided, *I'm tired. I can't do this any longer.* I had some pain meds I kept in my backpack from a knee surgery I had, and I just took the entire bottle. I was finally DONE. Every pain that I held in my life just burst open, and I just couldn't take it. I was in immediate despair. I decided that October 26, 2017 was my last day on earth. For every pill I took out the bottle as I sat in the car, I thought about the heartache, disappointments, rejections, all the people I tried to love, people who I tried to help, people who lied and talked about me, the picture of my son on his headstone, my best friend who was the sister I always wanted that was killed, the rape and molestations and being silent for years, and when the pain of my life continued, the bottle was now empty. I sent a few text messages out to three friends, just giving them my funeral instructions. The next thing, I woke up at the hospital. I wasn't *dead*. The doctors said I had consumed liters of Tramadol that should have shut down my system within an hour.

The doctor who was head of the unit came in to talk to me and ask me what happened. I explained to him what I wanted to do and why. He handed me three sheets of papers. He told me to write one letter to God, one to my son, and one to myself in the future. He explained the letter to God was to repent for my actions and thank Him for His grace and mercy. The letter to my son was to say goodbye to him, but I have to move on in life because it's killing me and to apologize for not living for him. The letter to my future self was to say I'm sorry for trying to stop the progress, not knowing how great I would become. As I sat and wrote these letters in front of this doctors, tears streamed down because I didn't know how hopeless I was. When I was stable enough, they planned to move me to a behavioral mental hospital called Mesa Springs. They called my friends and family to let them know what was taking place, but they wouldn't allow me to see anyone. Then, I was transported to Mesa Springs.

What Happens at Mesa Hospital Can't Stay There

I entered Mesa Hospital afraid and uncertain. I didn't know what to expect at all. The procedures were stated and made known. I knew I was there involuntarily. I couldn't use my cell phone, and no one could see me for a few days. I was afraid and alone. I walked into this place not knowing anyone but needing so much help. After all, who would try to kill themselves after everything in life tried to? I just knew something was wrong. The staff at Mesa Springs welcomed me and made me feel so comfortable. They never judged me from day one. They explained why they took our cell phones and why we only had twenty minutes of talk time a day to speak with family. I was just so frightened.

When I went to my first therapy session and explained everything I could get out through all the sobbing, my therapist said stunned, "You made it this far?" I thought it was a statement, but it was a question. She said, "I'm surprised you haven't tried to kill yourself a long time ago."

Then I laughed and asked, "Was I too late?"

Then, I went into my group session and had to tell them the same things I told her in private. They had the same response. I then knew, I wasn't this unstable person, but a person who had bottled up years and years of so much pain, until the bottle finally burst open leaving me open and exposed with no place to go. These hard places and dark places throughout my life were not just accidents or things that just happened. They were all planned to get me to where I am now.

Internal Terrorist Attack

I have been part of a terrorist attack that started when I entered the world, and now every bomb, hidden or unhidden, was exploding all at once inside my mind. Unresolved issues, the seeds planted by others, the seeds I planted, the seeds Satan planted, all developed into core beliefs. A core nuclear weapon that had been set up to wipe me completely out. The first bomb was planted on me when I entered the world; it was called rejection, and it attached itself to two teenagers who were fooling around at prom and were rewarded with a rejected baby neither of them wanted because they were babies themselves. The bomb inside of me grew because it attracted other seeds such as unlovable, being less than, not worthy, and limitations. These seeds had wrestled with my soul when I entered the world and were watered by life, pain, hard places, and lack of knowledge. They all kept them fed and growing.

But as the terrorist of our soul is planting seeds at the beginning, God planted only one seed called Life that grows when it first encounters the Light. The Light—Jesus Christ—reminded me in the chapel to remember Job. I would bypass it and continue to feed what was hungry in my soul, pain. Then one day, as I sat in my room in Mesa Springs, I began to question myself about what I remembered about Job from the Bible, and I compared him to me. I said, talking to God, "Well, when God sits you in a place of stillness, you have no choice but to seek Him for answers to tough questions." So, I said, "Well God, here is my chart."

<u>JOB</u>
Blameless
Wealthy
Repented for his kids
Moral of good standards
Wouldn't curse God
Friends turn on him
Health was tested
Kids died
Wife wasn't right after her loss
<u>Dee</u>
Not blameless (I am now in Christ)
Not wealthy (My father is rich in heaven)
I pray for my kids
Only lost one, not several
I try to keep moral standard, but I fail at times
Have not cursed God, but did questioned
Plenty of friends and family turned their backs on me
Health tested
One husband went crazy and tried to kill me

My list got longer than Job's, and I didn't understand why God wanted me to remember him. Because remembering him made me more depressed over what I had endured. Then the Holy Spirit told me to go back and read Job again. And the first thing I couldn't get past was that

Satan was doing what he does, prowling the earth, and *God offered up Job*. I was like, *What?*

Chapter 4: The Offer

Job 1:8
Then the Lord said to Satan, "Have you considered my servant Job? There is no one on earth like him; he is blameless and upright, a man who fears God and shuns evil."

Why? Why did the offer even take place? Now, I understand God is God. He can do what He wants, when He wants. But I needed to know why He offered Job, because my real question was why had He offered up me? Better yet, have you considered why he has offered you? Have you considered (taken notice of or paid attention to) my servant? It's like God put the spotlight on us and yelled to Satan, "Right here! This is her. This is him. Have you considered this one?"

I call God Pops at times, so I said, "Pops, now why would You offer me up to endure all the pain I went through, and I'm sure I have some more in the future? I know You collect my tears and You know our pain. But surely, You don't offer us up." It's hard to believe that a loving God would place you on center stage and tell Satan do what he wants, but you can't kill them. *Why?* This is when I found out the offer was just a selection to greatest and it was from a pure love that only comes from God.

As I go back throughout my life, I can see that even though an event seemed unfathomable at the time, the afflictions was God's love is unfailing creating good in my life. The lessons that came from each of the events of my life strengthened my faith. I didn't see myself being anywhere near Job, because, from the beginning, Job trusted God and knew that His purpose was more important than anything he had. I wasn't there back then, but I have arrived there now. I realize that each event and situation brought me to a greater trust in God and a deeper relationship with God. The offer up for Satan to attack our lives in areas is not to destroy us, but to discipline and bless us through the process. Discipline is never comfortable, and it doesn't feel good. It can feel like we are being torn apart, and we literally are. We are being torn apart in areas we are weak in, where we had setup idols, where we are being disobedient. It is all just to strengthen our relationship with God for what's to come.

I remember when I got out of Mesa Springs, I felt so free and so afraid because I didn't want to go back into a place of darkness. Mesa Springs had become a safety net for me to be me. I would cry in the days leading up to being release to my therapist out of fear of what would await me on the other side. I didn't want to face people with their judgements or answer questions. I wanted to remain free from all the hurt and pain. I wanted it to be just me and God, with no distractions. I finally understood most of all the whys in my life and why He chose me to endure. All of it was discipline, but He choose me because He knew how I would respond. God knows us. God told Jeremiah 1:5 (MSG), "Before **I** shaped **you i**n the womb, **I knew** all about **you**. Before **you** saw the light of day, **I** had holy plans for **you**: A prophet to the nations— that's what **I** had **i**n mind for **you**." We are no different from our brothers and sisters in the Bible. Every verse speaks life and instructions to us. If He knew Jeremiah, He knew all about us. Pause, right here and say those words: "God knew me, and He knows me now." Say this until it goes deep down in your heart and you feel His presence and a tear begins to form. Truth sets us free. When I think about how He knew all about me, all about us, before we entered our mothers' wombs, my soul rejoices because it confirms that He offered us up to be used because He knew we would be victorious. If it wasn't so, God has the power to prevent everything from happening; He knew the outcome.

Our human minds can't comprehend the things of God. Our minds tend to be very limited when we think God wouldn't allow this and that to happen. However, He tells us in Romans 8:26-28 (MSG),

Meanwhile, the moment we get tired in the waiting, God's Spirit is right alongside helping us along. If we don't know how or what to pray, it doesn't matter. He does our praying in and for us, making prayer out of our wordless sighs, our aching groans. He knows us far better than we know ourselves, knows our pregnant condition, and keeps us present before God. That's why we can be so sure that every detail in our lives of love for God is worked into something good.

The offer is to work us into something that is good for His kingdom. As of today, I'm forty years old. When I reflect on every detail of my life and what's to come, everything is woven together for my good. Yes, certain situations almost took the breath out of me, but it was for my good. One person asked me how I feel about God at forty years old. I responded by saying, "I feel as though I'm finally getting to know Him." Like any important relationship, all trials either grow or break the relationship, and with His grace and mercy, my relationship with Him has grown. I remember thinking I would never recover from my son's passing. As of today, I can talk about him, look at the pictures, and remember all the good things about him. God was patient with me through it all. He allowed me to vent and pull away at times, but He still loved me and never forsook me. I wouldn't be anywhere near the person I am today if my trials in life hadn't happened.

The offer produced so much that can't be completely written. What did the offer produce in you? If it produced good fruit such as loving others more, giving more, having more patience, having more understanding, being more forgiving, and your faith has increased, then the offer of you worked for God's glory. But if it produced bad fruit such as bitterness, anger, malice, and confusion, then it's time to rid yourself of the false beliefs that created bad fruit that hinder you from living in freedom. Satan is a great manipulator in helping us create these beliefs such as, God doesn't love us, so He allowed all these bad situations to happen to us. We believe the lie, and thus it produces seed that stop us from being effective in our lives and the kingdom of God. He wants us to think God offered us up to be destroyed. That is completely a lie. God didn't offer Job up because he was a bad person. Many of our brothers and sisters in the Bible went through several situations and not all for discipline. Look at our joint-heir, our Lord and Savior Jesus Christ. What did He do to be persecuted and killed? He had the power to avoid it all, but His love for us allowed Him to deal with whatever came His way. He never sinned, but He suffered on our behalf for God's purpose. We, too, are part of His purpose. No one on earth has experienced the torture Christ did; our trials are minimal compared to His, though we sinned and He didn't. God knows what His purpose in our lives is and how valuable we are to it. "Any means necessary," I always hear God say, when He is breaking me in areas of disobedience.

After I figured out that we are all offered up to be set apart in so many ways, I thought it was the end of all the tough pains in life. But, no! Months after Mesa Springs, I connected when a guy I met when I was seventeen. Through the years, we had never run into each other until we both were divorced and hanging around the same events. I was so free, that on our first little date at a coffee shop, I felt like a free teenager with my feet crossed in a chair. I felt as though I could walk on water. My relationship with God was so close, I was healed from the past, and I only wanted to live life to the fullest. Over the years, for some reason, this man would always come up in my mind. We never had sex when we were younger, but he would always come in my mind. I always thought he was the most handsome guy I knew, his personality was great, he was successful in business, and now he loved the Lord and was working for God in the church. It was so weird because when I was talking to him, my soul said, *Finally*. I finally felt safe with a guy. My heart felt safe. I told him everything. Things I didn't tell my ex-husband in the past. I finally felt that "finally" in my spirit. So, I prayed and ask God what He wanted me to do. God responded to love him unconditionally. I was like, cool, I can do that, but I wasn't prepared I think for what was to come.

We started off so good. We would read the Bible together, travel, and work on projects together. He is and was my first pure love. I could be myself, and I was free from the hurt and pain of my past. I thought this was the one my soul had waited for all my life. I would get lost in hearing him teach me about life and experience. One day, we were having lunch, and he started to cry telling me how good God had been to him. To see him cry was another level for me. I saw him vulnerable and his gratefulness towards God. I would tell him, "You are perfectly imperfect for me." There was nothing I wouldn't do for him. He owned a business, and we decided to remodel it. We would work all day and then head to work on our project until 12 or 1 a.m. He was the first man I was all in for. The first man I didn't have any walls up with.

But, Mother's Day 2018, I woke up at three in the morning to go his house. His front screen was open, and his front door was only pulled to. He had a key to my home, and he showed me where he kept his key for his home so we both have access to each other homes at any time. I walked in, and I saw a pair of women's high-heeled shoes in the living room. When I walked up stairs, he was running down with a robe on, but I pushed by him, only to see a naked woman lying in his bed. His daughter was home from school, so to keep from waking her up, I whisper to him to come down stairs. He told the woman to leave, and I cried so hard, and I felt sick to my very being. What I thought was all a lie.

All of a sudden, I began to talk to him about his soul and salvation until the sun rose, then I left, shattered to my core. All the way home, I was questioning if all of it was a lie and why I discussed his soul after he had shattered my heart. I knew then I was truly a believer of Jesus Christ to put myself aside to minister to someone else's brokenness. He apologized, and I forgave him. But, it wasn't the truth. Everything got worse. He continued to sleep with that woman along with others, and he started telling me that she and the other women he was sleeping with were better than me. I remember coming to his business, crying and explaining to him how bad he hurt me. He started laughing at me. I knew I wasn't nothing to him then. To laugh in my pain, penetrated my heart so deeply. But I kept hearing God say, "Love him unconditionally." However, there was nothing that man wouldn't say or do to me to break my spirit. As I write this now, my heart welts with pain of how I was treated.

One day, I made a list of all the things said and done to me to be able to express to him how he hurt me. After I sent it, we talked on the phone, and he explained to me for over two hours how he would never leave any of his women for a person like me. He started the crucifixion of my soul all over again; it felt like I was being beaten with words, and I was just weeping. Through that, though, I asked, "What did I do wrong but try to love you unconditionally?" I remember the silence on the other end of the phone. I was dedicated to God and trying my best to love and now this. I realized that words from people had a greater impact than deeds done. Satan had me rehearsing everything he was saying to me, until my seizures started back, depression creeped in, my hair started to shed, and I wasn't eating or sleeping; I was back to suffering in silence. I only confided in a few people, and when I confided the first time, they became so angry towards him that I couldn't get wise counsel any longer. As more things were said and done, I would just take it to God and try my best not to let it seep into my soul. I realized the guy I had fallen in love with was broken and didn't have the capacity to love me. It was all based on pretending to be healed, but he wasn't. Hurt people hurt others; sometimes it's intentional, and sometimes they don't realize how they are inflicting pain because they have become accustomed to the pain they're in. I also realized not to judge him, because I too could inflict the same pain if I didn't seek God with all my soul to be delivered from the pain. Pain is a vicious cycle, and if we are not careful, we will become a casualty of a war that we never had any part of. He was where I used to be in pain, but I had turned to another path so I wouldn't damage someone else's life.

I felt like if I didn't try to help him see the goodness of God, then I wasn't loving him enough, but he didn't love me. I believe he had a care for me as a human being, at times. However, love was far from me with him. He loved the women on the path he was on. He respected them because they loved him being broken, and they could feed off his brokenness with sex, money, neediness, and anything else that was draining from his due to his insecurities. I just wanted him healed and following the path God had set out for him. I could see the anointing on his life and how he had so much influence, that if he changed, he would draw so many souls for the kingdom of God. I couldn't make him see or accept me as me. I wondered why I was offered up in this situation, I still wonder as of today. I got peace by knowing I did what was required by loving him unconditionally and that he saw a character of God that he may not have seen from a woman that was pure. I never asked him for anything, and I only wanted us to be in Christ.

I evaluated recently why this relationship was so hurtful. It was on the same scale with me losing my son. I know you may be thinking, *How? It was only a guy, and hearts are broken all the time.* That is true. However, it was the place of safety, and I was in the Lord that connected the two. When my son died, I felt so at peace with God living according to His way. When I met Him, I was healed and living according to His way. Both places in my heart, I felt safe with God, but both situations left me vulnerable and unsure of who I really was. Then, the Holy Spirit reminded me of all the trials He has delivered me from and how He has never forsaken me. I understood sometimes we are offered up in a situation, not for self, but for others to know Him the way we do. I know I left an impact of how God's grace, love, and mercy is because most people wouldn't put forth an effort and minister to his soul. During this time, I had so many people upset with me and attacking me saying I didn't know my worth and more. I knew exactly who I was; I knew what God could do when we open ourselves up to allow Him to do it. I was being longsuffering in love, so an opening could happen.

I use to think God used people in the strangest way to accomplish His purpose. Do you remember when He told Hosea to marry a prostitute in the Bible? Hosea's wife would leave, and God would tell him to go back and get her. The purpose was to show the nation how we were prostituting towards God by serving idols. The lesson I learned was that each person's will is dependent on what they want for their own lives. I want a path of God's way because I know what the other path will lead to. The offer up that God sends us in is always for His purpose, and He knows exactly what we will endure; and I'm thankful for even this situation with the guy because I learn so much more about myself and God. Also, the relationship connected me to his family, especially his mother and stepfather, who welcomed and loved me outside of my connection with him. I called his mother and father my Godparents because God added them to my life right in time. I gained so much insight for listening to them, because they provided wise counsel. I gained a new family, beautiful sisters, aunts and uncles, and cousins that genuinely love me and a new church family, as well. Satan assumed he would take away my life by afflicting my soul, but through my endurance in trusting God, I gained an entire family outside of my afflictions. God knows what the offer will bring about in our lives. He has holy plans for us and great expectations. But to get to those great expectations, we have to bury dead things for the past and present.

Chapter 5: Burying Dead Things

Have you ever planned a funeral or done the preparation for the funeral of a loved one? It's a tedious process of several decisions. My aunts have been in the funeral home service for many years, and I have heard many of the stories of the burial process. I was also part of the burial process for my son. Before burying my son, I never knew so many decisions needed to be made, such as, selecting a cemetery with different plot choices; the types of services the funeral home offers; the types of caskets to choose from; the clothing the deceased is to wear; the order services for the program, which includes selecting singers or reading of scriptures. There is a process immediately when the person is declared deceased. The funeral home is contacted, and the body is prepped and embalmed, while the loved ones are planning the order of service. Then the funeral happens, followed by the trip to the cemetery, and finally, the repass for family and friends to eat together. The day is filled with so many emotions.

The way we bury our loved ones is the same way we have to bury our past mistakes, pain, or anything that doesn't fit into our future. I was in so much pain when my son died, and it took a lot of time to let go of the negative emotions associated with his death. But one day, I told myself that when dead things die, after a few days an odor comes, and it affects everything that comes in contact with it. My pain and emotional baggage had been carrying an odor for years, and the smell had drowned out any good aroma. So, I decided I must bury all the dead things in my life for good and only reflect on lessons learned from a positive perspective.

I had to remind myself that my future couldn't contain life and death at the same time. To begin the process of burying dead things, I started speaking the Word of God to everything that was stinking up my life. The more we speak opposite of the smell of the negative thoughts, the more our mindset will start to change. Light will begin to shine brighter, and the aroma of God will begin to seep out of us. The process is a lifelong process. It's not something that happens over night because the longer we live in the world, the more we will experience because we are constantly afflicted. We must learn to rid ourselves quickly of the toxic, so we can live life in abundance. With all the plans I had in life and all the detours, several dead things were on me. I must confess, those I realized were present on me then are still at times present on me. Here is my list; maybe you can identify with some or all of them:

Abandonment
Fear
Not good enough
Bitterness
Anger
Undeserved, intentional wickedness towards me

These were my luggage, and at times, a few still try to rise up from the grave, so I have to set my mind on the Word of God to keep them buried. This is how we know the dead things of the past are not buried or are not buried deep enough: either we think about the situation, and the emotions are still there, or something similar happens, and it reminds us of what happened before.

Let me explain what happen to me, when I realized I was carrying stinky things. When I was younger—maybe between the ages of seven and nine— I was an only child, and I was home alone most of the time. Because of this, I had this habit of calling my mother, my aunts, and just whomever would answer the phone. At the time, I didn't know how adults conducted their life, but I remember there would be times when they were too busy to talk, and their tones would confirm it. Instantly, I started to feel that I was bothersome and not important, so I isolated myself as a kid. Well, as an adult, I contacted a guy I was dating, and he answered the phone as though hearing my voice irritated him. I immediately shut down and started apologizing for calling and decided if he wanted to talk, he would need to contact me after that. I felt just as I did at the age of seven. The dead thing was stinking because of the way I internalized it. Now, I'm not saying the reactions were justified or if how I felt was justified. But as an adult, I too have answered the phone frustrated, not towards the person that is calling, but it's just that when I answered, I was in a frustrating situation outside of them. I loved them and wanted to talk to them, however, my tone reflected they were irritating. Now, I'm cautious of how I handle calls and text messages because I know how it feels to be on both sides now. This example is just a small one but relevant one for me, because this dead seed birthed several other things, such as bitterness and anger towards people that didn't know they offended me and anger towards myself for not expressing how situations made me feel.

Recently, I've been told, feelings don't matter, however, they matter when it's valid. I agree, feelings or emotions shouldn't control all decisions because they are temporal. However, if you belittle me by words, and I'm offended; then as a result, I may cry and be hurt, which are valid. If a person continues, then the behavior will warrant a placement on my block list because now I'm allowing you to abuse me by remaining in your presence.

Long story short in this chapter, this is the process of how I buried or continue to bury dead things. First, I identify what the dead thing is by writing it in my journal. I list the dead thing and the situation it appeared in. Then, I write the emotion that is tied to it. After that, I search the Bible (the Word of God, which is the absolute truth), and I write what the Lord says about me. Then, I write what the Word of God says in my journal, on my bathroom mirror, and on an index card to place it on my dashboard. I willfully don't put energy into resurrecting the dead thing. I affirm and repeat what God says over the dead thing to keep it buried and to produce more life inside of me. This may seem easy. However, how deeply the action or deed has penetrated determines how much of our will we must use to force ourselves to repeat the process to be made whole. Here is an example below (this is a true entry in my journal):

10-01-2018

(Dead Thing) I'm not good enough. (Situation) He told me, I would never leave anyone of my women you found out about to be with someone like you. You are the bottom whore on my totem pole. (Emotion) Pain, disrespected, not appreciated, rejected, cried for days. (The Lord Says) You are more precious than rubies. Who can find YOU. Your husband will gain favor from me when he finds you. You are a Royal Priesthood. When I created you, I said it was GOOD.

Now, you may be thinking, *Sussssss... I know that is not what this guy told you.* Yes, He did. I remember calling my mother crying, and she said, "I don't know why what others says is valuable to you." She didn't understand that when you have been beyond kind to someone, for that response to be your reward, that is what cut deepest. I knew that everything he said was lies from the pit of hell. However, love leaves you vulnerable to whatever is to come. Ephesians 6:12 tells me, "For our struggle is not against flesh and blood, but against the rulers, against the authorities, against the powers of this dark world and against the spiritual forces of evil in the heavenly realms." Satan and his powers can use anyone we love. It was a guy then, but it can be family or kids next. I forgave so many times because that's what the scriptures told me to do. I searched all the scriptures that God had spoken and inserted myself in the scripture. David became Dee, Job became Dee, Ruth became Dee, and so on. I spoke about these things until the dead things were six feet under and the enemy was my footstool.

This may seem simple, but when you have more than one dead thing you are carrying, you will use up many journals, you will not be able to see in your bathroom mirror, and your dashboard in your car will look like a poster board. However, it *works* because there is nothing but truth and power in the Word of God. In order for things to die, life or the energy that is used to fuel it must be destroyed. Who has the power to destroy everything we can ever imagine? God. He tells us how to bring down strongholds in His Word. That is what a dead thing is, a stronghold. A thought that has bound our mind, contrary to what God has said about us.

Most of the time, the dead things are words said to us. Have you noticed you can remember every negative thing someone has said but barely remember the good? I thought long and hard about this, and I believe the reason why we remember the negative is because it contradict what has been already decreed; so, when it enters us, it becomes a debate, and depending on our foundation, our wounds, and our relationship with God, we decide what will stick. This can happen vice versa. If we have been told only negative things all our lives and God sends someone to deposit good, a debate is started; and depending on those things listed, we decide what will stick. *However*, this is what I love about the Lord: when you belong to Him, everything always works out for our good. The bad, good, and ugly work out for our good for those who are called according to His purpose. I just want you to know that dead things will stink up your life, but they no longer have to. We are equipped by the anointing of Jesus Christ to bury those things and keep them where they belong and not bring them into our future. It's hard to love purely with bitterness, it becomes a mess. In John 10:6-10 (MSG), we read,

Jesus told this simple story, but they had no idea what he was talking about. So he tried again. "I'll be explicit, then. I am the Gate for the sheep. All those others are up to no good—sheep stealers, every one of them. But the sheep didn't listen to them. I am the Gate. Anyone who goes through me will be cared for—will freely go in and out, and find pasture. A thief is only there to steal and kill and destroy. I came so they can have <u>real and eternal life, more and better life than they ever dreamed of</u>."

I love this scripture because it says a "real and eternal life, more and better life than [we] ever dreamed of." I can't imagine obtaining that type of life if I am still thinking the same, doing the same, being the same, and hanging at the same places with the same people.

I forgot to mention, dead things don't have to be something inside of us; they can be people who are zombies in your life or places we attend. People can drain the life out of us if we let them. I don't know if I can mention this or not. I heard a pastor once say , "We need to stop bleeding on other people." Have you ever had a great day, and the someone calls you with all their issues? Now, they don't want to pray about it, and they don't want you to give them scriptures to read. They only want to vent and, instantly, their frustration, dread, or disgust has you feeling the same way. One day, I accidentally replied, "Geesh, I was good until ten minutes ago when I answer this call." I was being truthful, but my tone was drained. Have you walked into a place, and instantly felt depressed? I have also. Burying dead things means we bury all things that prevent us from living an abundant life. I had to realize through pain, that if a person doesn't want my presence in their life, they will become dead and stink up my life. So, at that moment, I have to decide who must live, and I have to decide *now*. I'm not allowing nothing or no one to kill my purpose and zeal for Christ.

The second thing I do when burying dead things, after I have journaled and spoke words of affirmation from the Word of God, is I pray without ceasing for God to help me stay away from anything that reminds me of what broke me or placed dead things in me in the first place. I've come to realize that we can only do *anything* with the power of God, not on our own, because our flesh is weak. Several times, after this guy had broken my spirit and challenged my mind, I went back for more. Each time it ended up worse than before. His words would feel like sharpened daggers piercing my soul. I remember one day as I sat crying on my couch, an image of a heart with pinholes of flowing blood appeared. The Holy Spirit told me, "This is what your heart looks like. Your soul's bleeding; *stop* the bleeding." Even after the Spirit of God spoke to me, I still didn't disconnect myself. When I look back, I see all the ways of escape that God afford me, and to this day, I shed tears thinking that I could have started the process of healing a long time ago.

The third thing I do is that I confide in wise godly counsel, a Christian therapist. I've learned that confiding in friends and family can cost you your peace, because friends and family are mostly biased, and they never forget, even after you have forgiven. They will remind you every time you bring that person's name up what they did and how they felt about it. Also, out of their emotions and their experience, they give advice that is sometimes not aligned with the Word of God. They will have you locked up in jail with how to handle situations. So, to avoid vain babbling and an arrest record, I started consulting a counselor faithfully once a week or every two weeks. Having a Christian counselor is helpful because they have a foundation on the Word of God, but they have combined it with a strategy to help us along with the process. Also, the counselor is not familiar with the other party, and they are by oath sworn not to tell your business. So, when you leave your counseling session, you can rest assured in knowing you are only a client and no one knows how damage you are and how much work is needed.

Now, when we bury our loved ones, we normally go and place flowers on their tombstone or have some type of memorial for them. This is what I do with some the dead things that I have buried. If I *decide* to memorialize them, it's only to reflect on the goodness of God and how His grace and mercy kept me from the reactions and being delivered from them. We don't memorialize the dead things to rehearse the pain and to keep us stuck by being angry with people or ourselves. I learned this the hard way by rehearsing every painful moment in my life until I was at Mesa Springs. I learned the hard way again in my thirties by allowing built-up pain to have me outside in the front yard attempting to fight a guy over his bad behavior towards me, while I'm a full adult with grandkids in total humiliation, due to my lack of self-control. This public moment made we realize I wasn't healed and I had to truly forgive because the anger was pouring out of my heart. When we know it's truly buried and we are fully healed, we will feel a release. When we talk about it to others, peace and gratefulness will lead the testimony.

Chapter 6: Set Apart

I have told y'all my many plans I had, what I feared the most, my dark and hard places, why I think he offers us, and why we should bury dead things we carry. Now we are at why we are set apart. It literally took me forty years to understand *I don't fit in* with certain people. Believers don't fit in with the world. Also, True Believers don't fit with Carnal Christians; we can get along at times, but not consistently. It's clear why believers don't fit into the world in 2 Corinthians 6:14-18,

Do not be unequally yoked with unbelievers. For what partnership has righteousness with lawlessness? Or what fellowship has light with darkness? What accord has Christ with Belial? Or what portion does a believer share with an unbeliever? What agreement has the temple of God with idols? For we are the temple of the living God; as God said, "I will make my dwelling among them and walk among them, and I will be their God, and they shall be my people. Therefore go out from their midst, and be separate from them, says the Lord, and touch no unclean thing; then I will welcome you, and I will be a father to you, and you shall be sons and daughters to me, says the Lord Almighty."

True (mature) Believers and Carnal Christians are the same because of the core belief, however, the mature believer is a consistent doer of the Word of God. It's a difference. When I was doing my own way, I was never comfortable, but I could tolerate worldly things more than when I'm walking on the path of righteous. After a while, I quickly retreat to who I am. I always felt like God has His children on one of those toddler cords, so we can't get too far out there before He yanks us back into where we are supposed to be, which is right by His side and working out our soul salvation with trembling and fear.

Some people think I'm strange in many ways, some may be good, and others can't describe it. I've been this way *all of my life*. I have been waiting to turn forty for forty years, I mentally feel like I'm in my fifties already. I have always felt a lot older mentally but looked a lot younger. I started life early, and God gradually increased me with wisdom as He drew me closer to Him and I endured the lessons from life. My plan was to release this book at my fortieth birthday because I felt that I have endured the wilderness part of my life, and now I'm entering the promised land. But because I was distracted by other desires, my plan failed. But God's plans prevailed. I believe with all my heart, this is the reason why I was set apart for this very moment in my life.

This is what I've learned, the Bible tells us to be holy throughout. When we think of holy, we often think of holiness as being perfect. However, we will never be perfect. The Bible says our very best actions are like filthy rags. Isaiah 64:6, "All of us have become like one who is unclean, and all our righteous acts are like filthy rags; we all shrivel up like a leaf, and like the wind our sins sweep us away." In Hebrew, the word "holy" is Qodesh and the root word is Qadash which means "to set apart for a specific purpose" (Ancient Hebrew Lexicon, virtualbookword.com,publishing, Jeff Benner). We can't be perfect without God's help, but we can be holy by being set apart for a specific purpose. 1 Peter 2:9 tells us, "But you are a chosen race, a royal priesthood, a holy nation, a people for his own possession, that you may proclaim the excellencies of him who called you out of darkness into his marvelous light." When I read this scripture, knowing now that I'm not seeking the perfection of being a holy nation but seeking Him with my being to be used for His purpose, the heaviness of imperfection was freed of me. God knew we couldn't do it alone so He sent his Son, Jesus Christ, to save us from ourselves and to restore our relationship with Him.

Being set apart is the love of God, and it has always been in existence. I used to get upset when people would reject me, but I realize God knows the entire story of my life, and He knows who needs to play a role and who doesn't. When rejection happens, I learned to rejoice because God allowed it for my protection and His purpose. Have you heard of someone trying to fit a square peg into a circle slot? Ok, that is us, when we try to fit in where we just *don't belong*. I've tried it a few times, and it always ends up an epic failure. What also happens is the people or situation we try to fit in with or into begin to feel like we are being judgmental, or that we think we are better than them. The truth is we are better than *no one,* but we are better than the situations we allow in our lives.

True story: There is a new thing called situationship, where no one is committed, and everyone is free to date everyone, have sex with anyone, and that's about it. Marriage is not part of the forecast; no titles are given. It's just that. What happens though is, when you have standards, trying to be a part of this will *always* fail because you can't fit in, so the people involved will use manipulation, deception, or make it seem so innocent to bring you into the situationship because they know being truthful from the start, middle, or at any point will cause you to run off. So, they use everything they have learned about you, including God, to draw you into this situation, and once you are so far in, the light is turned on and you realize, everything is pretend. Now, in their mind, they are thinking they are winning all along because they got you to accept the situation by whatever means they used. The only person that is never considered is God. The game they're playing is not with you, but with God. Being set apart brings about protection at all costs, including heartbreak. I'm not judging anyone for their choices in life; I'm just giving you my perspective on what was in my life for a period. It was two worlds constantly warring against each other and a lot of evil tactics done. During this time, I was praying, fasting, and having all kinds of dreams, but I prayed my influence and the presence of God in me would shift the situation. Then, I heard that influence will not change a person's character. That statement became real in my life. I was personally attacked so many times about me being so different in a negative way that God had to catch me from being depressed all because I wouldn't willingly be part of the game. I know now that God sets us apart from many situations in life, because He truly loves us. He loves us so much He would rather for us to suffer a heartbreak temporarily than to see us die in sin. He loves us so much to move us over to the side and fight our battles so we want occur the blows we would occur if we were fighting on our own. Love hides us under His wing so we can take refuge and heal in our darkness, so no one but Him can see how badly damaged we are.

Do *you* truly know , there is *no one* like *you*? That your life is for a specific purpose that is assigned only to you? No one can beat you as being you. I had to write that in my journals lots of times. When God created you, He took time to number the hairs on your head, to pour the number of tears you would need, to breathe the number of breaths it would take to survive this world to enter into His eternal kingdom. Set apart is an understatement to who we are. We are the chosen people of God. We are His children; the joint heirs of Jesus Christ. Our brother is both Lord and Savior. We have a Father in heaven that fills every position in our lives. He can use our enemies for His purpose.

Set apart by love is just that. Love separated us to give us life now and later. The way we can fully accept this type of love is to accept that we are purposed to be different, which is our true selves. We can't be cloned, and we are irreplaceable. I started valuing who I am when I understood that I'm a rare ruby that can't be duplicated. I'm cut too differently to be replicated. *You are too!* I have arrived to the point that as long as I'm a vessel for God for His glory, the opinions of others don't matter. My grandmother had a china cabinet, and she would put the fine china plates along with expensive glasses there. When I was young, I only knew I couldn't touch the cabinet or open it and touch anything in the cabinet. She would, every now and then, wipe the dust off every item in the cabinet and close the cabinet back up. There were only a few occasions when she would use the china and glasses; it was for important guests. The guests knew how to handle the china plates and glasses. They would place the glasses down with care. The plates weren't moved until she picked them back up. She would take her time washing the dishes and drying them instantly and quickly placing them back in the cabinet. We are the fine china and expensive glasses in the china cabinet, only to be used and adored by people designed to handle us with care. Not for daily use; the moment we lower our value, we become a paper plate—disposable at any moment to all who don't value themselves.

Job, along with many of our brothers and sisters in the Bible, were set apart for a specific purpose. When we read the book of Job, we know that His story was to show us that God has all power and nothing that happens in our lives is done without him approving of it. We know that God will use pain and suffering to destroy thinking; Job's friends thought that he was suffering due to sin in his life. But God prove to them, that is not always the case; it rains on the just and unjust. Job's life was for us to see how God operates and how Satan is limited in his power. Satan doesn't get the response from Job he hoped for, Job never cursed God because he knew God had the power to do whatever He chooses, and his faith in God healed and restored him. How will our end be?

Chapter 7: Victory is Assured - We Win

Job 42:10
When Job prayed for his friends the Lord restored his fortunes. In fact, the Lord gave him twice as much as before!

Oh my God! Did you see it coming? We didn't see the big picture? I imagine us sitting on a porch in older age, maybe at eighty or ninety, saying these things. "I didn't know that right around the corner from that situation was victory." Listen, I can't contain it while I'm writing to you. I know most, or some, are saying, "I can't believe this chick told us her business," and some of you may be thinking, *Why?* I'm telling what my life has been the last forty years, so you can witness the victory of entering into the promises of God.

I only gave you the highlights of my life thus far. As of today, I must tell you about the victory that is assured to us. It's guaranteed if we faint not by remaining obedient in faith. Years ago, I couldn't have ever imagined writing a book and being healed over situations in my life. Some days I wonder, *What if I would have been successful in taking my life?* Then, this book would have never been written. No one can tell our story but us. Not only did I get to write this book, but I was able to see my grandkids be born, my kids grow up, and my cousins grow up. I met new people who love me genuinely. I have peace that surpasses all understanding that God released in my life. I'm healthy physically. When I open my eyes every morning, God is the first person I talk to, because it's amazing how He regulates the body while sleeping that I don't die while I sleep. I still struggle with certain areas of my life, but God has been so present to me, that I keep handing Him all my issues. I finally understand what moves God's heart. It's obedience, which is the core of faith. When we obey, we are saying with our heart that we trust God by faith in what he asks us to do. After forty years of wilderness, the most powerful lesson is obedience by faith.

I went years doubting God in many situations, hearing from God through His word, but allowing myself and Satan to talk me out of the Lord's path for my life. From the beginning to end of the Bible, obedience is at the core of many of the prophets and disciples. One day, I was studying the Bible because my pastor quoted Psalm 27:13, "I remain confident of this I will see the goodness of the Lord in the land of the living." He is eighty-one years old and has been preaching for fifty-nine years as of today. When he preaches, he every scripture he says challenges me to go read the Scriptures myself. Well, I like to read the entire chapter once given a scripture. He adopted me as his granddaughter, and sometimes he calls me little GH, which are his initials because he says I remind him of himself when he started learning the Scriptures. I began to read Deuteronomy 28 about disobedience and obedience. Below are the scriptures in the NIV Bible. This chapter has been powerful in my growth with understanding the keys we have been given and how faith works.

Deuteronomy 28: Blessings for Obedience

1 If you fully obey the Lord your God and carefully follow all his commands I give you today, the Lord your God will set you high above all the nations on earth. **2** All these blessings will come on you and accompany you if you obey the Lord your God:

3 You will be blessed in the city and blessed in the country.

4 The fruit of your womb will be blessed, and the crops of your land and the young of your livestock—the calves of your herds and the lambs of your flocks.

5 Your basket and your kneading trough will be blessed.

6 You will be blessed when you come in and blessed when you go out.

7 The Lord will grant that the enemies who rise up against you will be defeated before you. They will come at you from one direction but flee from you in seven.

8 The Lord will send a blessing on your barns and on everything you put your hand to. The Lord your God will bless you in the land he is giving you.

9 The Lord will establish you as his holy people, as he promised you on oath, if you keep the commands of the Lord your God and walk in obedience to him. **10** Then all the people on earth will see that you are called by the name of the Lord, and they will fear you. **11** The Lord will grant you abundant prosperity—in the fruit of your womb, the young of your livestock and the crops of your ground—in the land he swore to your ancestors to give you.

12 The Lord will open the heavens, the storehouse of his bounty, to send rain on your land in season and to bless all the work of your hands. You will lend to many nations but will borrow from none. **13** The Lord will make you the head, not the tail. If you pay attention to the commands of the Lord your God that I give you this day and carefully follow them, you will always be at the top, never at the bottom. **14** Do not turn aside from any of the commands I give you today, to the right or to the left, following other gods and serving them.

Curses for Disobedience

15 However, if you do not obey the Lord your God and do not carefully follow all his commands and decrees I am giving you today, all these curses will come on you and overtake you:

16 You will be cursed in the city and cursed in the country.

17 Your basket and your kneading trough will be cursed.

18 The fruit of your womb will be cursed, and the crops of your land, and the calves of your herds and the lambs of your flocks.

19 You will be cursed when you come in and cursed when you go out.

20 The Lord will send on you curses, confusion and rebuke in everything you put your hand to, until you are destroyed and come to sudden ruin because of the evil you have done in forsaking him[a] **21** The Lord will plague you with diseases until he has destroyed you from the land you are entering to possess. **22** The Lord will strike you with wasting disease, with fever and inflammation, with scorching heat and drought, with blight and mildew, which will plague you until you perish. **23** The sky over your head will be bronze, the ground beneath you iron. **24** The Lord will turn the rain of your country into dust and powder; it will come down from the skies until you are destroyed.

25 The Lord will cause you to be defeated before your enemies. You will come at them from one direction but flee from them in seven, and you will become a thing of horror to all the kingdoms on earth. **26** Your carcasses will be food for all the birds and the wild animals, and there will be no one to frighten them away. **27** The Lord will afflict you with the boils of Egypt and with tumors, festering sores and the itch, from which you cannot be cured. **28** The Lord will afflict you with madness, blindness and confusion of mind. **29** At midday you will grope about like a blind person in the dark. You will be unsuccessful in everything you do; day after day you will be oppressed and robbed, with no one to rescue you.

30 You will be pledged to be married to a woman, but another will take her and rape her. You will build a house, but you will not live in it. You will plant a vineyard, but you will not even begin to enjoy its fruit. **31** Your ox will be slaughtered before your eyes, but you will eat none of it. Your donkey will be forcibly taken from you and will not be returned. Your sheep will be given to your enemies, and no one will rescue them. **32** Your sons and daughters will be given to another nation, and you will wear out your eyes watching for them day after day, powerless to lift a hand. **33** A people that you do not know will eat what your land and labor produce, and you will have nothing but cruel oppression all your days. **34** The sights you see will drive you mad. **35** The Lord will afflict your knees and legs with painful boils that cannot be cured, spreading from the soles of your feet to the top of your head.

36 The Lord will drive you and the king you set over you to a nation unknown to you or your ancestors. There you will worship other gods, gods of wood and stone. **37** You will become a thing of horror, a byword and an object of ridicule among all the peoples where the Lord will drive you.

38 You will sow much seed in the field but you will harvest little, because locusts will devour it. **39** You will plant vineyards and cultivate them but you will not drink the wine or gather the grapes, because worms will eat them. **40** You will have olive trees throughout your country but you will not use the oil, because the olives will drop off. **41** You will have sons and daughters but you will not keep them, because they will go into captivity. **42** Swarms of locusts will take over all your trees and the crops of your land.

43 The foreigners who reside among you will rise above you higher and higher, but you will sink lower and lower. **44** They will lend to you, but you will not lend to them. They will be the head, but you will be the tail.

45 All these curses will come on you. They will pursue you and overtake you until you are destroyed, because you did not obey the Lord your God and observe the commands and decrees he gave you. **46** They will be a sign and a wonder to you and your descendants forever. **47** Because you did not serve the Lord your God joyfully and gladly in the time of prosperity, **48** therefore in hunger and thirst, in nakedness and dire poverty, you will serve the enemies the Lord sends against you. He will put an iron yoke on your neck until he has destroyed you.

49 The Lord will bring a nation against you from far away, from the ends of the earth, like an eagle swooping down, a nation whose language you will not understand, **50** a fierce-looking nation without respect for the old or pity for the young. **51** They will devour the young of your livestock and the crops of your land until you are destroyed. They will leave you no grain, new wine or olive oil, nor any calves of your herds or lambs of your flocks until you are ruined. **52** They will lay siege to all the cities throughout your land until the high fortified walls in which you trust fall down. They will besiege all the cities throughout the land the Lord your God is giving you.

53 Because of the suffering your enemy will inflict on you during the siege, you will eat the fruit of the womb, the flesh of the sons and daughters the Lord your God has given you. **54** Even the most gentle and sensitive man among you will have no compassion on his own brother or the wife he loves or his surviving children, **55** and he will not give to one of them any of the flesh of his children that he is eating. It will be all he has left because of the suffering your enemy will inflict on you during the siege of all your cities. **56** The most gentle and sensitive woman among you—so sensitive and gentle that she would not venture to touch the ground with the sole of her foot—will begrudge the husband she loves and her own son or daughter **57** the afterbirth from her womb and the children she bears. For in her dire need she intends to eat them secretly because of the suffering your enemy will inflict on you during the siege of your cities.

58 If you do not carefully follow all the words of this law, which are written in this book, and do not revere this glorious and awesome name—the Lord your God— **59** the Lord will send fearful plagues on you and your descendants, harsh and prolonged disasters, and severe and lingering illnesses. **60** He will bring on you all the diseases of Egypt that you dreaded, and they will cling to you. **61** The Lord will also bring on you every kind of sickness and disaster not recorded in this Book of the Law, until you are destroyed. **62** You who were as numerous as the stars in the sky will be left but few in number, because you did not obey the Lord your God. **63** Just as it pleased the Lord to make you prosper and increase in number, so it will please him to ruin and destroy you. You will be uprooted from the land you are entering to possess.

64 Then the Lord will scatter you among all nations, from one end of the earth to the other. There you will worship other gods—gods of wood and stone, which neither you nor your ancestors have known. **65** Among those nations you will find no repose, no resting place for the sole of your foot. There the Lord will give you an anxious mind, eyes weary with longing, and a despairing heart. **66** You will live in constant suspense, filled with dread both night and day, never sure of your life. **67** In the morning you will say, "If only it were evening!" and in the evening, "If only it were morning!"—because of the terror that will fill your hearts and the sights that your eyes will see. **68** The Lord will send you back in ships to Egypt on a journey I said you should never make again. There you will offer yourselves for sale to your enemies as male and female slaves, but no one will buy you.

I don't know if you paid attention. But the disobedience scriptures are longer than the obedient scriptures. The blessings are clear for obeying, and curses are clear for when we disobey. To have a life where victory is assured, we must obey. We win when we obey God's commands and His will for our lives. Obedience is the most essential element in our spiritual lives. From the beginning, mankind's relationship was broken with God due to disobedience. In a article a read on a website (https://watv.org) it stated the following ;

"The Bible defines perfect faith as 'faith joined by works or actions,' not just the verbal expression of one's belief (Jas 2:14–26)." In this context, "actions" means by obedience to God's word. Faith can be measured through obedience. Obedience is the visible expression of invisible faith. Jesus also set the example of obedience when He came to this earth to save mankind" Hebrew 5: 8-10, "Although he was a son, he learned obedience from what he suffered and, once made perfect, he became the source of eternal salvation for all who obey him and was designated by God to be high priest in the order of Melchizedek. Jesus is God Himself—Everlasting Father—by nature, but He came to this earth by making Himself the Son of God and lived a life of faith in perfect obedience to God (Isa 9:6; Php 2:5). The Bible says that Jesus learned obedience from what He suffered and was

made perfect. Without obedience, our faith cannot be made perfect. The book of Romans also emphasizes that obedience leads mankind to salvation. Romans 5:18-19, "Consequently, just as the result of one trespass was condemnation for all men, so also the result of one act of righteousness was justification that brings life for all men. For just as through the disobedience of the one man the many were made sinners, so also through the obedience of the one man the many will be made righteous. It is impossible for us to obey God alone. However, when Christ lives in us, obedience is easy. Jn 14:21 "Whoever has my commands and obeys them, he is the one who loves me. He who loves me will be loved by my Father, and I too will love him and show myself to him. Obedient faith is vital to keep God's commandments. Without obedience it is impossible to keep them. "Jesus has also said that only those who do the will of God will enter heaven. Mt 7:21, "Not everyone who says to me, 'Lord, Lord,' will enter the kingdom of heaven, but only he who does the will of my Father who is in heaven. Faith and obedience are [indivisible], and faith can be proven through obedience. If a [person] is confident in his[/her] faith but disobeys God's word, he[/she] cannot be said to have faith." (https://watv.org)

Obedient Faith is why I wrote this book. I started this book years ago and would add to it gradually. It was delayed due to disobedience, but through God's discipline, I was able to finish it without distractions. This book is not just a representation of myself, it represents anyone who has been tested or is being tested and doesn't know how their story will end. I didn't know either. I started out with so many plans that seemed right, and some could still happen according to His will. What I feared the most happened to me, only to be later the best thing God could have done because it delivered me from false sense of control over my life. My kids being idols to fill love in my life, I learned to value time, that God will never forsake us, and that He is always present. The dark and hard places taught me that darkness can be my finest hour and that darkness is a development state which provides safety. In this place, God's dealt with things that are within me. I couldn't appreciate light until I had experience darkness. The offer is because God trusted me to respond to how He has created me to be, and it's for my good. Burying bad things, I carried set me free to receive all the blessings of God by freeing up space in my soul. Being set apart is for His specific purpose for my life. With all these summed up, I just want you to know that victory is *ours* on this side of heaven and eternally. John 17:17, "Sanctify them in the truth; your word is truth!"

1 John 5:4, "For everyone who has been born of God overcomes the world. And this is the victory that has overcome the world—our faith"

Revelation 12:11, "And they have conquered him by the blood of the Lamb and by the word of their testimony, for they loved not their lives even unto death." Every relationship and situations I describe this book was restored with my ex's finding their purpose in this life and us remaining good friends. I realize what the enemy meant for evil, God meant it for good. We all learned from our experience and I firmly believe that everything was meant for my good.

We must remain in obedient faith to the very end to receive the blessings of God in this world and in the next to come. Trials and sufferings will continue, but if we remain in Him by faith, we are assured that we have the victory on both sides of life. Let's live this life out in victory by obedient faith to accomplish the purpose of God for His glory! We win together!

Journal Your Process

Offered Up to Be Set Apart

Journal Your Process

Acknowledgements

Writing a book is harder than I thought and more rewarding than I could have ever imagined. None of this would have been possible without friends and family, who encouraged me to finish the book, and the people who propelled me into greatness: Tee, Zee, Monty, my mother Sharon, Aunt Daine, Uncle James, Dedric, Queundra, Charsiney, Aunt Stephanie, Dajuana, Cheryl, Josh, Lyndia, Lawrence, Mrs. Linda, Mr. Isaac, Brother G, and Dawn.

I'm eternally grateful to my uncle Charles Jones (Big Uncle Charles), who taught me about scriptures and who would daily remind me what God's requirements are for my life. You were the best person I've ever met, and I wish you were present to read and see what you seeded into my life. You loved me unconditionally, even though we were not blood-related, but connected by the Spirit and marriage. Words can't express what you taught me about life and how to treat people by your example. Rest in peace.

To my family. My kids: Tee, Zee, and Monty. To my Mama, Sharon; Aunt Daine; Aunt Michelle; Uncle James; Aunt Stephanie; and Uncle Charles—thanks for always being consistent people in my life and always believing in me. The entire Jones Family; there are too many to name. We took that scripture on multiplying serious. Thank you to the Malone Family, the Evan Family, and the Johnson family for accepting me.

In loving memory of Harvey Jones, Juanita Kimble, Rosie Lee Jones, Christopher (Deuce), Archer Perry Janice Perkins, Patrick Jones, and Charles Jones.

Reference

Retrieved information Feb 21,2020, from (https://watv.org)

Retrieved information February 02,2020, from Ancient Hebrew Lexicon, virtualbookword.com, publishing, Jeff Benner.

www.ingramcontent.com/pod-product-compliance
Ingram Content Group UK Ltd.
Pitfield, Milton Keynes, MK11 3LW, UK
UKHW022220230426
12048UKWH00016BA/972